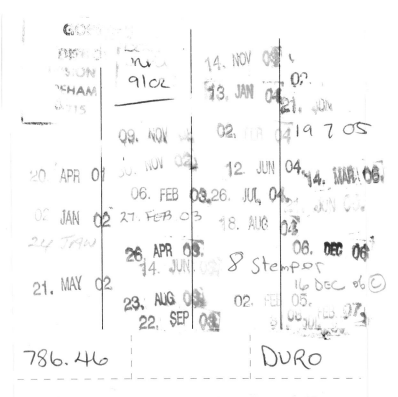

JazzCollection

FHM

WISE PUBLICATIONS
London / New York / Paris / Sydney / Copenhagen / Madrid / Tokyo

Exclusive Distributors:
Music Sales Limited
8/9 Frith Street, London W1V 5TZ, England.
Music Sales Pty Limited
120 Rothschild Avenue, Rosebery, NSW 2018, Australia.

Order No. AM965790
ISBN 0-7119-8339-9
This book © Copyright 1998 by Wise Publications.

Compiled by Peter Evans.
Music arranged by Stephen Duro.
Music processed by Allegro Reproductions.
Cover design by Michael Bell Design.
Photograph (Duke Ellington) courtesy of Redferns.
Printed in the United Kingdom by Caligraving Limited, Thetford, Norfolk.

Your Guarantee of Quality:
As publishers, we strive to produce every book to the highest
commercial standards. The music has been freshly engraved and the book has been carefully designed
to minimise awkward page turns and to make playing from it a real pleasure.
Particular care has been given to specifying acid-free, neutral-sized paper
made from pulps which have not been elemental chlorine bleached.
This pulp is from farmed sustainable forests and was produced with special regard for the environment.
Throughout, the printing and binding have been planned to ensure a sturdy,
attractive publication which should give years of enjoyment.
If your copy fails to meet our high standards, please inform us and we will gladly replace it.

Music Sales' complete catalogue describes thousands of titles and
is available in full colour sections by subject, direct from Music Sales Limited.
Please state your areas of interest and send a cheque/postal order for £1.50 for postage to:
Music Sales Limited, Newmarket Road, Bury St. Edmunds, Suffolk IP33 3YB.

www.musicsales.com

| Contents

Bernie's Tune

By Bernie Miller

Moderately bright

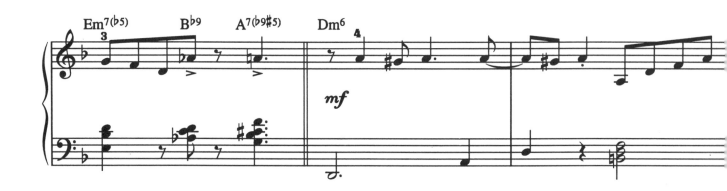

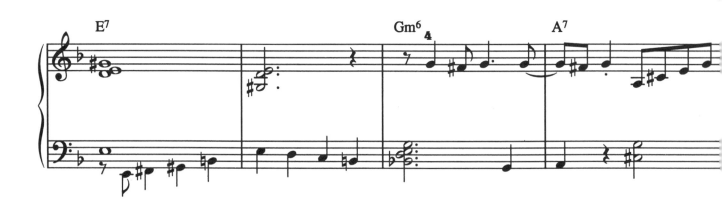

East Of The Sun (And West Of The Moon)

Words & Music by
Brooks Bowman

Me To The Moon (In Other Words)

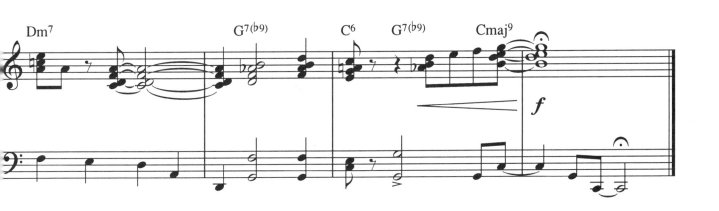

13

I Wish I Knew How It Would Feel To Be Free

Words by Billy Taylor &
Dick Dallas
Music by Billy Taylor

I Should Care

Words & Music by
Sammy Cahn, Axel Stordahl
& Paul Weston

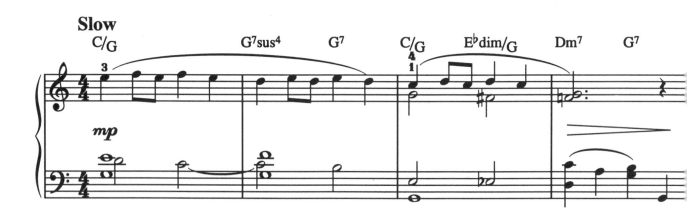

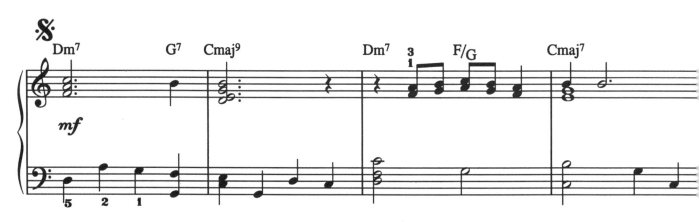

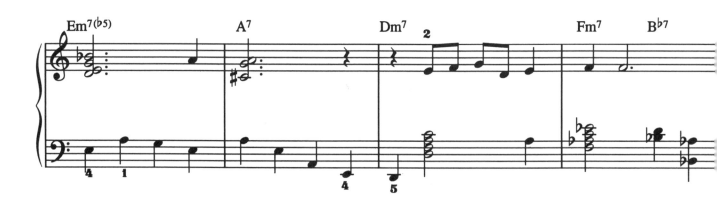

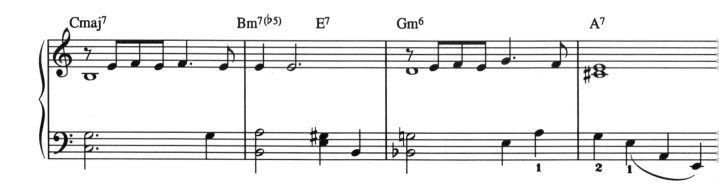

Beginning To See The Light

& Music by
mes, Duke Ellington,
Hodges & Don George

Moderately bright

21

Lullaby Of Birdland

Music by George Shearing
Words by George David Weiss

It Could Happen To You

Music by Jimmy Van Heusen
Words by Johnny Burke

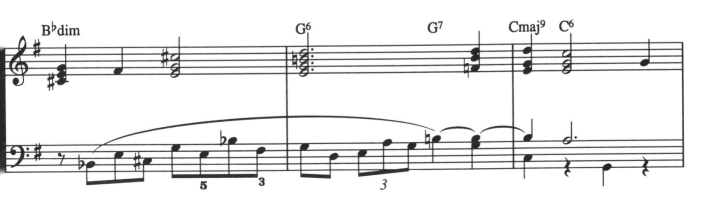

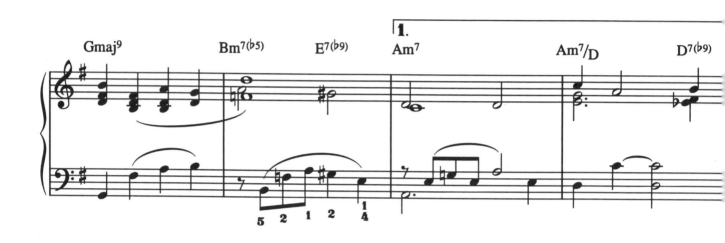

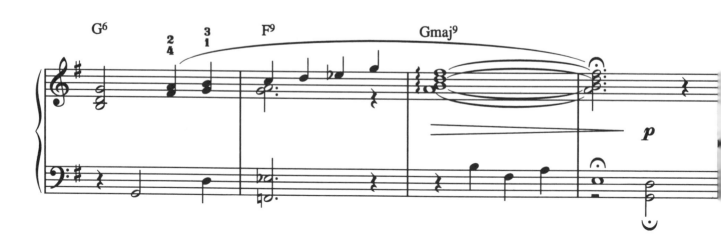

ude To A Kiss

& Music by
llington, Irving Gordon
: Mills

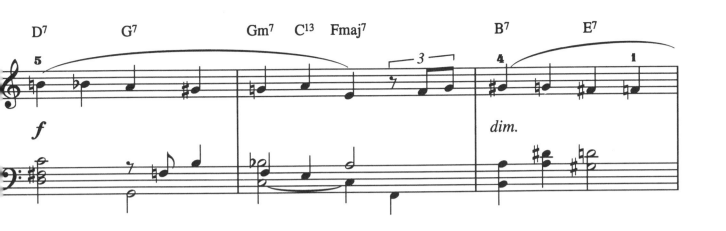

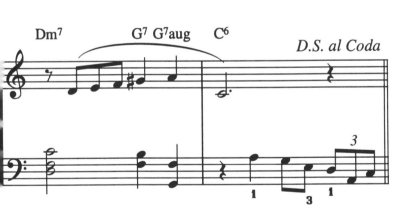

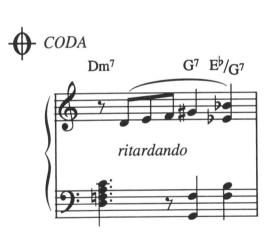

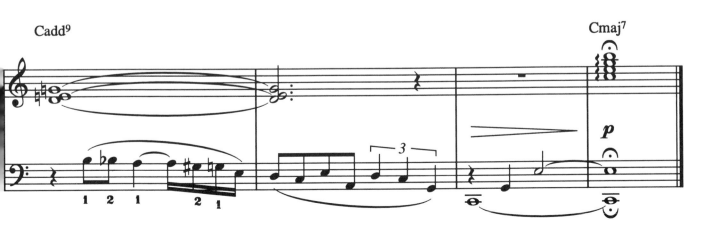

Perdido

Music by Juan Tizol
Words by Harry Lenk
& Ervin Drake

Moderately bright

34

Stella By Starlight

Music by Victor Young
Words by Ned Washington

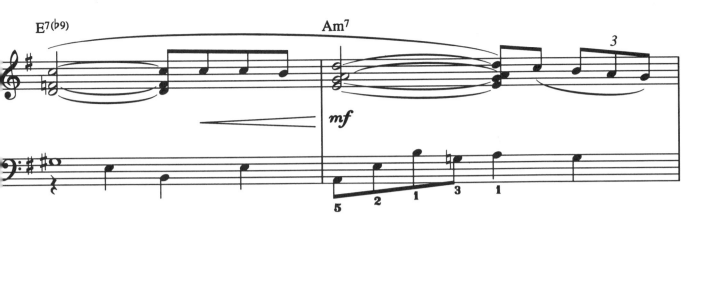

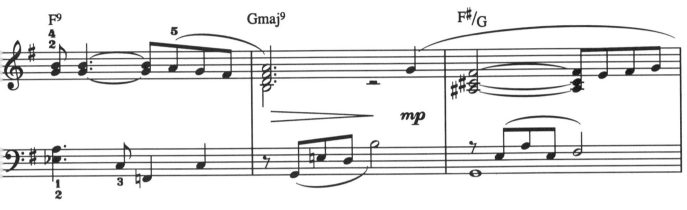

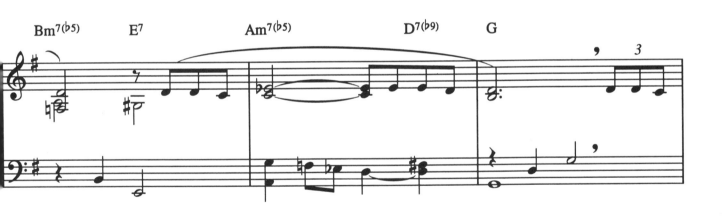

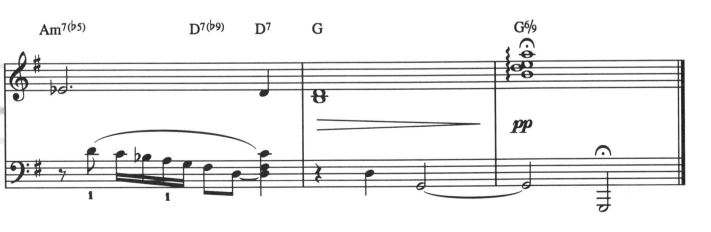

Take The 'A' Train

Words & Music by
Billy Strayhorn

Violets For Your Furs

Words by Tom Adair
Music by Matt Dennis

You Brought A New Kind Of Love To Me

Words & Music by
Sammy Fain, Irving Kahal &
Pierre Norman Connor

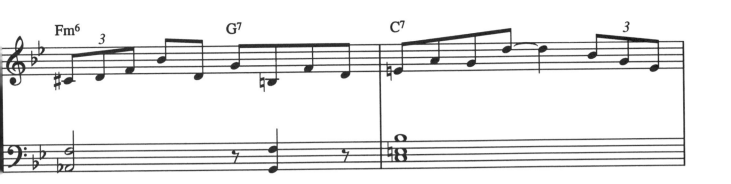

D.S. al Coda

Satin Doll

Words by Johnny Mercer
Music by Duke Ellington &
Billy Strayhorn